Have fun with Arts and Crafts

Fairies

Rita Storey

FRANKLIN WATTS
LONDON•SYDNEY

This edition 2013

First published in 2012 by
Franklin Watts
338 Euston Road
London NW1 3BH

Franklin Watts Australia
Level 17/207 Kent Street
Sydney NSW 2000

Copyright © Franklin Watts 2012
All rights reserved.
Series editor: Amy Stephenson

Packaged for Franklin Watts by Storeybooks
rita@storeybooks.co.uk
Designer: Rita Storey
Editor: Nicola Barber
Crafts: Rita Storey
Photography: Tudor Photography, Banbury
www.tudorphotography.co.uk
A CIP catalogue record for this book is available
from the British Library.

Printed in China

Dewey classification: 745.5
ISBN: 978 1 4451 2692 0

Cover images Shutterstock (top left), Tudor Photography, Banbury

Franklin Watts is a division of Hachette Children's Books,
an Hachette UK company
www.hachette.co.uk

Before you start

Some of the projects in this book require scissors, paint, glue
and a sewing needle. When using these things we would
recommend that children are supervised by
a responsible adult.

Contents

Sparkly Fairy Wand

Make fairy magic with these glittery heart and star-shaped wands. Add a touch of fairy dust to make your wishes come true.

For a sparkly wand you will need

- glittery card
- scissors
- sparkly pencil – if you don't have a sparkly pencil use an ordinary pencil and paint it or wrap ribbon around it
- gift ribbon
- glue and spatula
- glitter glue
- sparkly stick-on shapes
- pencil
- satin ribbon
- sticky tape

1 Cut out two identical heart or star shapes using the templates on pages 30 – 31.

2 Tape the pencil and some lengths of gift ribbon on to the back (non-glittery side) of one of the shapes.

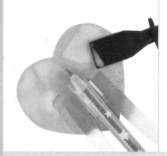

3 Spread glue all over the shape around the pencil.

4 With the glitter side on the outside press the second shape on top, sandwiching the pencil in-between. Leave to dry.

5 Decorate the wand with sparkly shapes and glitter glue to make it look really magical.

6 Make the gift ribbon curl by wrapping it tightly around a pencil and pulling it out through your fingers.

7 Finish your wand by tying a pretty bow with the satin ribbon, leaving long ends.

Wave your wand to make some good fairy magic.

Wand Magic

In fairytales, magic wands are often used to grant wishes. In the story of Cinderella the fairy godmother uses her magical powers to transform Cinderella's rags into a ballgown and glass slippers. With another wave of her wand she turns a pumpkin and two white mice into a coach and horses.

Flower Fairy Tutu

Every fairy needs a beautiful tutu as part of her outfit. This pretty skirt will magically transform you into a fabulous fairy. If you want a tutu that sticks out around your waist, keep the lengths of fabric quite short. If you want your tutu to float as you dance, you will need to cut longer strips of fabric.

For a fabulous tutu you will need

- tape measure
- 1cm wide ribbon – long enough to go around your waist plus 1m extra
- sticky tape
- 5m of voile or tulle (net) fabric, 25cm wide (you can buy this in craft shops – choose your favourite colour or use a few different colours.)
- scissors
- tiny stick-on jewels, sequins, bows or fake flowers to decorate

1 Measure 50cm from one end of the ribbon and tie a knot. Now measure 50cm from the other end and tie a second knot.

2 Stretch the ribbon out on a table or work surface. Using sticky tape, tape the ends of the ribbon to the work surface.

3 Decide how long you want the skirt of your tutu to be. Measure this length from your waist with the tape measure. Now you need to cut strips of fabric **twice** that length. Each strip should be about 7cm wide. If the ends of your strips are a bit wobbly you can trim them, or make them round to look like petals.

4 Fold one of the fabric strips in half from end to end. Now push the folded end under the ribbon somewhere between the two knots.

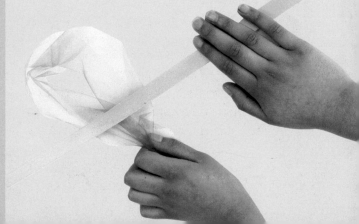

5 Thread the two loose ends of the strip through the loop in the fabric above the ribbon. This is a bit fiddly but it gets easier once you have done a few.

6 Slide the loop along so that it is close to one of the knots in the ribbon. Pull the ends of the fabric through to fasten the strip tight on to the ribbon.

7 Repeat steps 4 – 6, adding more lengths of material and sliding each loop along so that the strips of fabric are next to each other. When you reach the second knot your tutu is nearly finished.

8 You could decorate your skirt with tiny stick-on jewels, sequins, bows or fake flowers. To wear your tutu, tie the ends of the ribbons around your waist in a pretty bow.

If you have any fabric left over you could make a matching tutu for your favourite fairy doll. You will need a narrow piece of ribbon and some short lengths of fabric.

Do a beautiful fairy dance to show off your new tutu.

Ballerina Tutus

Ballerinas wear dance skirts called tutus when they perform classical ballets. Long, floaty skirts are called romantic tutus. Short, flat 'pancake' tutus stick straight out from the ballerina's hips. The **Dance of the Sugar Plum Fairy** is one of the most famous ballet dances in the world.

Gossamer Wings

Fairies are very proud of their beautiful wings. This pretty pair will have you floating on air.

For beautiful fairy wings you will need

- sheet of A3 paper
- ballpoint pen
- scissors
- sticky tape
- cling wrap
- tissue paper
- white glue mixed with about the same amount of water
- spatula
- strip of strong card
- hole punch
- 2 x 1m lengths of ribbon
- glitter glue

To make these wings you will need to use the table or work surface for at least two days. Before you begin, check that it is not needed for anything else.

1 On the A3 sheet of paper draw the shape of a pair of fairy wings (see template on pages 30 – 31). Cut the shape out and tape it down.

2 Stretch cling wrap over the table or work surface to cover the wing shape completely. Tape the cling wrap down.

3 Cut or tear the tissue paper into lots of pieces. The pieces can be different shapes and sizes. Fairy wings can be all one colour – or lots of different colours and patterns.

4 Glue the torn tissue paper pieces to the cling wrap to cover the shape of the wings. Overlap the pieces. Keep pasting on the paper pieces until you have three or four layers completely covering the wings, with no gaps.

5 Leave the tissue paper pieces to dry completely. This will take hours so leave them at least overnight. The wings should not be at all sticky when you touch them.

6 Carefully peel the tissue paper wings off the cling wrap.

7 Take the wing shape from under the cling wrap and lay it on the tissue paper. Draw round the wing shape.

8 Cut out the wings from the tissue layers.

9 Cut a piece of card roughly the same depth as the centre of your fairy wings and about 3cm wide. Punch two holes in the top and bottom of the card. Thread one length of ribbon through the top holes and the other length through the bottom holes. Turn your wings over and glue the card down the centre of the back. Leave to dry.

You can decorate your wings with glitter glue to make them even more sparkly.

Tie on your wings and you are ready to flutter, just like a real fairy!

Butterfly Wings

Real butterfly wings are beautiful and very fragile, just like fairy wings. See if you can find some pictures of pretty butterflies. Pick your favourite to help you choose your colours.

Glittery Snowflakes

Fairies love winter because of all the glitter and sparkle. They like to dust the gardens with frost and cover everything with a layer of shimmering snow. One of their jobs is to design all the snowflakes, every one with a different pattern. That is a lot of work! You can help them out by designing some snowflake patterns to make a window display.

For glittery snowflakes you will need

- squares of white paper in different sizes
- scissors
- glue and spatula
- silver glitter
- newspaper
- sticky tape

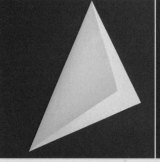

1 Fold one of the squares of paper in half diagonally.

2 Fold it in half again to make a smaller triangle.

3 With the long side of the triangle at the bottom, fold one corner over as shown above.

4 Fold the left-hand side over the top to make the shape shown in stage 5.

5 You will now have a triangle with two points sticking out. Cut off the points.

Snowflake Patterns

All snowflakes have six points, or six sides. Some are needle-shaped and others look like ferns. But it's true, every single snowflake that falls is different from all the others.

10

6 The shape should now look like the one in the picture above.

7 Cut small pieces out of the folded edges on both sides.

8 Carefully open out the snowflake and lay it flat.

9 Cover the snowflake with glue and sprinkle on some glitter. Tape the snowflakes to the window with the glitter-side against the glass.

Here is another great way to use snowflake cutouts. Use small pieces of sticky tape to fix the snowflakes loosely to a large sheet of white paper. Dab glue all over the snowflakes, including the cut-out parts. Dust the whole picture with glitter. Peel off the snowflakes. You will be left with white snowflakes on a glittery background.

Every sparkly snowflake you make will have its own special pattern.

Woodland Fairy Crown

Woodland fairy princesses love flowers. They wear crowns made from the beautiful flowers that grow in gardens and hedgerows. This pretty crown of paper flowers will turn you into fairy royalty.

For a royal crown you will need

- pipe cleaners
- 8 large sheets of tissue paper in different colours
- scissors
- ruler

1 Twist two or three pipe cleaners together to make a ring that fits your head.

2 Cut one sheet of tissue paper into squares 12cm by 12cm. Stack six squares on top of each other.

3 Fold 2cm of the tissue paper stack over towards the middle. Crease along the fold.

4 Turn the paper over and fold the same edge 2cm back. Keep turning over and folding to make a fan shape.

5 Twist a pipe cleaner loosely round the middle of the fan. Fold the paper fan in half. Use scissors to round off the ends of the tissue paper.

6 Open out both sides of the fan. Press down gently on the opened-out sides with your hands.

7 Carefully separate the layers of tissue paper one at a time to create a flower. Don't worry if you tear a layer or two.

8 When your flower is fluffed up, use the pipe cleaner to attach it to the pipe cleaner ring.

9 Repeat stages 2 – 8 to make more flowers in different colours. Attach them to the ring until it is covered in flowers.

Wear your beautiful crown and feel like the queen of the fairies.

Fairy Mischief

A long time ago, William Shakespeare wrote a play all about fairies. In the magical world of **A Midsummer Night's Dream** we meet Oberon the fairy king and his servant, Puck. The fairy queen, Titania, has four fairy servants, Peaseblossom, Cobweb, Moth and Mustardseed. When the play is performed, Titania and her fairy servants often wear crowns made of flowers.

Fairy Dream Catcher

Dream catchers are used by some Native American people to protect sleeping children. They believe that the woven threads across the middle are a bit like a spider's web – they capture bad dreams. This pretty dream catcher will catch any bad dreams and hold them tight. Only good dreams full of fairy magic will get through.

To catch some dreams you will need

- styrofoam frozen pizza base
- plate smaller than the pizza base
- bowl slightly smaller than the plate
- glue
- glitter
- scissors
- pencil
- embroidery thread in 3 colours
- embroidery needle
- beads and feathers

1 Draw round the plate on to the pizza base. Cut around the line you have drawn.

2 Draw round the bowl to make another smaller circle inside the big circle. Cut out around this smaller circle to make a ring.

3 Use the point of the pencil to make holes around the inner ring roughly 2cm apart and 5mm from the edge.

4 Cover one side of the ring with glue and dust with glitter. When it is dry, turn it over and cover the other side in glitter. Leave to dry.

5 Cut lengths of thread about 1m long. Tie one end of the thread to one of the holes in the circle. Thread the other end through the needle. Stretch the thread across the circle and through another hole.

6 Keep threading through the holes across the circle putting a bead on to the thread every now and again. When you are close to the end of the thread, tie it onto a hole. Repeat with the other lengths of thread until they are through all the holes.

7 Cut three more pieces of thread, each about 12cm long. Tie a feather to the end of each thread. Then thread a few beads on to the thread above each feather. Knot the ends to keep them in place.

8 Make three more holes near to the outside of the ring 6cm apart. Tie each piece of thread to one of the holes.

9 Using the pencil make a hole at the top of the dream catcher. Thread a length of embroidery thread though the hole. Hang up your dream catcher.

Hang your dream catcher in a window to welcome all the good dreams.

Fairy Tea Party

Fairies love dainty food. Hold a delicious mini tea party for your favourite fairy and her friends. You can make a bigger size of everything for yourself and your friends, too.

For a delicious tea you will need

Mini sandwiches
- 3 slices of bread, thinly cut and buttered
- your favourite sandwich filling (nothing too chunky)
- bread knife
- kitchen knife
- rolling pin

Mini meringues
- mini meringues
- cream
- raspberries

Fairy muffins
- mini-sized muffins
- buttercream icing
- kitchen knife
- sprinkles and chocolate chips
- raspberries and blueberries
- sweets
- small slices of cake

1 Make a sandwich with two slices of thin bread and butter and your favourite sandwich filling. Cut the slices into eight mini triangles.

2 Cut the crust off a slice of bread. Roll the bread with a rolling pin to flatten it a bit. Spread some filling onto the bread and roll it up. Slice the roll into tiny pinwheels.

3 Sandwich mini meringues together with a blob of whipped cream.

4 Top them with raspberries.

5 Buy or make some mini-sized muffins. Top them with a swirl of your favourite icing.

6 Roll them in sugar sprinkles or decorate them with chocolate chips.

7 Serve cakes whole or cut them into tiny slices.

8 Serve a selection of fruits such as raspberries and blueberries, sweets and tiny slices of cake.

Use a lacy handkerchief or a napkin as a tablecloth for your very best fairy china.

Invite all your friends to this yummy fairy picnic, mmmmmmmmmm.

Fairy Collage Picture

Fairies love pretty things. This collage of pretty pictures will add a touch of fairy magic to your bedroom. Start collecting lots of pictures of fairies and pretty things that you think fairies would like.

For a cool collage you will need

- fairy pictures cut from magazines, scraps of glittery fabric, flowers and other things that remind you of fairies
- large sheet of paper
- felt-tip pens
- scissors
- glue
- sequins, lace and glitter glue

For a tooth fairy box you will need

- small gift box
- sheet of white A4 paper
- coloured paper
- glue
- scissors and a pencil
- glitter glue

Fairy Collage Picture

1 Start a fairy scrapbox. Collect bits of pretty fabric, pictures cut from magazines, odds and ends of wrapping paper, ribbon and anything else you come across for your fairy collage.

2 Draw a heart shape on the paper the size that you want your finished collage to be. Cut it out.

3 Use the templates on page 31 to draw lots of pretty fairies. Colour them in and cut them out.

4 Starting with the bigger pictures, glue pictures, scraps and your fairy cut-outs on to the paper. Overlap the shapes and add the smallest ones last so they are not covered up.

5 When all the pictures are stuck down add some sequins, lace and a dash of glitter glue to complete your collage.

Your collage will look great pinned up behind your bed! You could create a smaller collage on a folded piece of card to make a fairy birthday card for one of your friends.

Tooth Fairy Box

1 Use the template on page 31 to draw a fairy on the white paper, small enough to fit on the side of the gift box. Glue the fairy shape onto the coloured paper. Cut an oval shape round the fairy.

2 Glue the picture on to the side of the box. Decorate round the oval with glitter glue.

Tooth fairy

If one of your teeth falls out wrap it in a tissue and put it under your pillow or in your tooth fairy box. In the morning the tooth fairy might have taken it and left you a coin in its place. The tooth fairy is very shy. No one has ever seen her.

3 Repeat the process to decorate the other sides of the box with more fairies.

Fairy Homes

These beautiful fairy homes will encourage fairies to come and live with you in your house or in the garden. Fairies are extremely shy, though, so you are unlikely to catch a glimpse of them.

For a fairy beach house you will need

- large plate
- kitchen foil
- demerara sugar
- small box
- card
- sticky tape
- scissors
- glue
- shells, pebbles, driftwood, twigs or spiky plants

For a gorgeous grotto you will need

- large plate
- kitchen foil
- a selection of things from the garden or park – moss, (available from florists or garden centres), leaves, twigs, bark, pebbles, cones
- thin coloured paper
- pipe cleaners
- glitter

A Fairy Beach House

1 Cover the plate with silver foil. Pour some demerara sugar on to the plate and spread it out to look like sand on a beach. Leave an area of silver foil for the sea. Add some pebbles and shells.

2 To make the beach hut, cut a hole out of the front of the box for the door. Paint the box in coloured stripes.

3 Cut two triangles of card and tape to the top of the box at the front and back (see picture). Cut a rectangle of card the length of the sides of the triangles plus 2cm. Shape the edges as shown. Fold it in half. Glue it over the two triangles leaving 1cm overhang on each side.

4 Finish off the beach house with shells, pebbles, driftwood, twigs and some spiky plants.

A Fairy Grotto

1 Cover the plate with silver foil. Spread the moss out, leaving a small area for a pond.

2 Use twigs to make a grotto that a fairy could use as a bedroom. Decorate the rest of the plate with pebbles, cones, leaves, twigs and bark.

3 Cut some simple flower shapes from the coloured paper. Push short lengths of pipe cleaner through the centres to make stems.

4 Use the pebbles and stones to make paths and banks.

You could add a touch of glitter to help the fairies find their way to the grotto.

The Cottingley Fairies

In 1917 two schoolgirls photographed fairies dancing in the trees and grass. The girls, 16-year-old Elsie Wright and her 10-year-old cousin, Frances Griffiths, claimed that the fairies in the photographs were real. Many people did not believe them, but there were many others who did. Sixty years later Elsie and Frances confessed they had created the pictures using cutouts of fairy drawings from a magazine. But although Elsie admitted that eight of the photographs were fakes, she said that one of them was taken by accident – and that it was a genuine photo of real fairies.

Sleeping Beauty Bed

The story of Sleeping Beauty tells how a bad fairy puts a curse on a baby princess that makes her sleep for many years. Your favourite fairy doll will get a good night's sleep and have sweet dreams in this pretty bed.

For a beautiful bed you will need

- rectangular tissue box
- two sheets of A4 paper
- felt-tip pen
- ruler
- scissors
- card – coloured or sparkly
- wrapping paper
- sticky tape
- fabric
- double-sided tape
- stuffing (cotton wool or kapok)
- glitter glue and stick-on jewels
- ribbon

1 To make the headboard draw round the end of the tissue box on one of your sheets of A4 paper. Use the ruler to add an extra 6cm on to the height. Cut out the shape.

2 Fold the paper in half. (It should now be half as wide as your box).

3 Use the template on page 32 to draw the shape of **half** the headboard on the paper. The centre of your headboard will be the line made by the fold. Cut out the shape. Open out the paper.

4 For the foot-board follow steps 1 – 2 but this time add an extra 4cm at the top of the shape. Use the template on page 32 to draw the shape of **half** the footboard. The centre of your footboard will be the line made by the fold. Cut out the shape. Open out the paper.

5 Use the paper templates to draw the headboard and footboard on to the back of the card. Cut them out.

6 With the hole and all the joins underneath, cover the tissue box with wrapping paper.

7 Use double-sided tape to stick the headboard and footboard on to the ends of the bed. Decorate with glitter glue and stick-on jewels.

8 To make the cover, cut a piece of fabric big enough to fit across the bed and down both sides. Stick on a piece of ribbon with double-sided tape and fold it back. Trim with a ribbon bow.

9 To make the pillow, cut out two rectangles of fabric. Use double-sided tape to stick down three sides.

10 Fill the pillow with stuffing.

11 Tape up the open side.

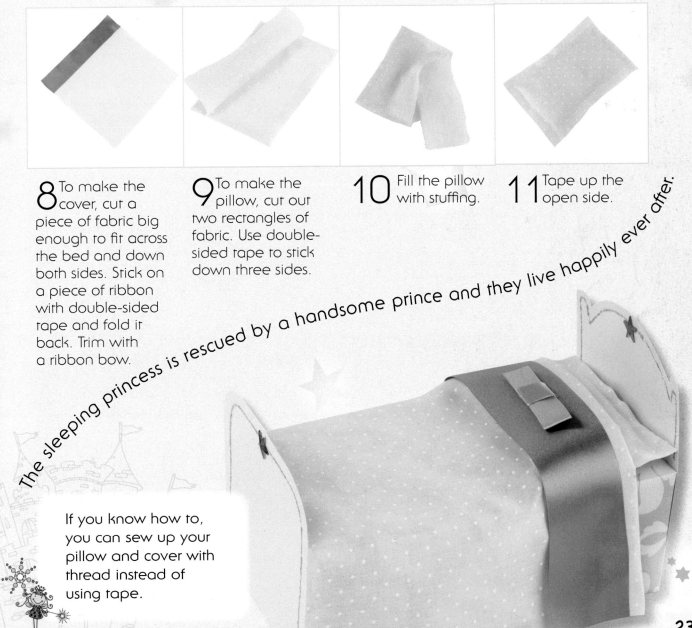

The sleeping princess is rescued by a handsome prince and they live happily ever after.

If you know how to, you can sew up your pillow and cover with thread instead of using tape.

Flying Fairies

This cute fairy mobile will look great on a windowsill. It could also be a table decoration – or maybe you could try hanging the fairies from your bedroom ceiling.

For your flying fairies you will need

- branch with small twigs
- paints
- paintbrush
- newspaper
- flowerpot
- modelling clay
- thin white card
- felt pen
- thin, patterned card
- thin pink card
- scissors
- double-sided tape
- cotton or embroidery thread
- needle

1 Paint the branch. Leave it to dry on the newspaper.

2 Paint the flowerpot. Leave it to dry on the newspaper.

3 When the paint is dry, decorate the flowerpot with a different colour. Leave to dry.

4 Push modelling clay into the bottom of the flowerpot. Push the branch into the modelling clay.

5 Use the templates on page 30 to draw the arms, wings, hands, head and feet. Cut them out.

6 Use the template on page 30 to draw three-quarters of a circle on the patterned card.

7 Pull the two straight edges together to make the shape into a cone. Stick down the edge with double-sided tape.

8 Stick on the arms, wings hands, feet and head.

9 thread the needle and tie a knot in the end of the thread. Push the threaded needle up through the centre of the wings from inside the cone. Use the thread to hang up the fairy. Then repeat steps 5 – 9 until you have as many fairies as you need.

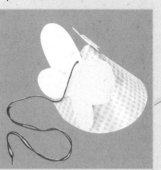

Fairy Flower Garden

Fairies love the sweet smell of flowers, and they are good friends with the bumblebees. In this colourful flower garden picture, the bumblebees are playing hide-and-seek in and out of the flowers.

For a flowery fairy garden you will need

- round objects of different sizes to draw round – jar lid, mug, coin, bottle top
- several sheets of coloured paper (for the flowers)
- pencil
- scissors
- glue
- green paper for stems and leaves
- large sheet of paper (for the background)
- yellow pipe cleaners
- brown pom-poms
- googly eyes
- yellow paper

1 Use the larger round objects (jar lid, mug) as templates to draw some different sized circles on the coloured paper. Cut the circles out.

2 Use the small objects (coin, bottle top) to draw a small circle on each large circle.

3 To make petal shapes, cut from the outside edge, stopping at the small circle as shown.

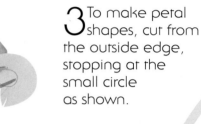

4 Glue the petals together to make a flower. Put the larger shapes at the back. Cut small circles of coloured card and stick them in the centre of each flower.

5 Cut out stems and leaf shapes from the green paper. Glue them on to the background paper.

6 Glue the flowers at the top of the stems.

7 To make a bumblebee, wind the yellow pipe cleaner round the brown pom-pom. Trim off any excess pipe cleaner. Stick on two googly eyes.

8 Fold a piece of yellow paper in half. Starting at the folded edge, draw a wing shape. Cut the shape out. Unfold the shape and glue it on top of the brown pom-pom. Make as many bumblebees as you need for your garden.

Your buzzy bees can fly around your pretty flowers. Buuuuuzzzzzzzzz.

'Pretty as a Picture' Frame

This pretty frame would make a lovely present. Fairies love animals, so use it to frame a picture of your pet or favourite animal, or cut out a fairy picture from a magazine to be the star attraction.

To make this pretty frame you will need

- felt-tip pen
- three A4 sheets of card
- scissors
- ribbons
- glue
- ruler

1 Draw a heart shape on the card using the template on page 32. Cut it out.

2 Cut out two squares of card 20cm x 20cm.

3 Cut strips of ribbon 40cm long. Glue the strips side by side on one of the squares of card. This is the front of the frame.

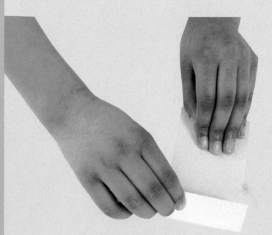

4 Cut a strip of card 4cm wide and 20cm long. Bend back 3cm to make a flap.

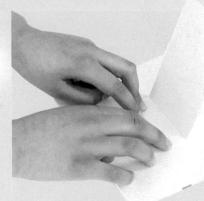

6 Fold the ends of the ribbons over the edge of the first piece of card and glue them in place. Now glue the front and back of the frame together with the ends of the ribbons in-between.

5 Glue the bent piece of card on to the other square of card in the centre. This is the back of the frame.

7 Glue the heart shape on the front of the card on top of the ribbons.

8 Cut a photograph into a heart shape slightly smaller than the one on the card. Stick it on the front.

What a purrrrrrrrrrrrrfect picture.

You can decorate your frame with scraps of lace or other trimmings.

Templates

Flying Fairies
Pages 24 – 25

Sparkly Fairy Wand
Pages 4 – 5

Gossamer Wings
Pages 8 – 9

Fairy Collage Picture
Pages 18 – 19

Sparkly Fairy Wand
Pages 4 – 5

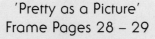
'Pretty as a Picture'
Frame Pages 28 – 29

Sleeping Beauty Bed
Pages 22 – 23

Further Information

Books

It's Amazing: Fairies by Annabel Savery
(Franklin Watts, 2013)

Dressing Up As A: Fairy by Rebekah Shirley
(Franklin Watts, 2013)

Websites

www.rainbowmagiconline.com/uk/

Index